that the violences committed by those who have tak...
arms in Massachusetts Bay, have appeared to me as th...
acts of a rude Rabble, without plan, without concert, &
without conduct, and therefore I th...
Force now, if put to the Test, wou...
them with greater probability of...
expected from a greater Army, if...
fered to form themselves upon a m...
acquire confidence from disciplin...
resources without which every thi...
of a single Action. In this va...
of The King's Affairs, it is t...
Servants in which His Al...
& essential step to be taken t...
ment, would be to arrest and...
& abettors in the Provincia...
appear in every light to be a...
regardless of your Proclama...
should presume again to assem...
poses; and if the steps taken upon this occasion be accom...

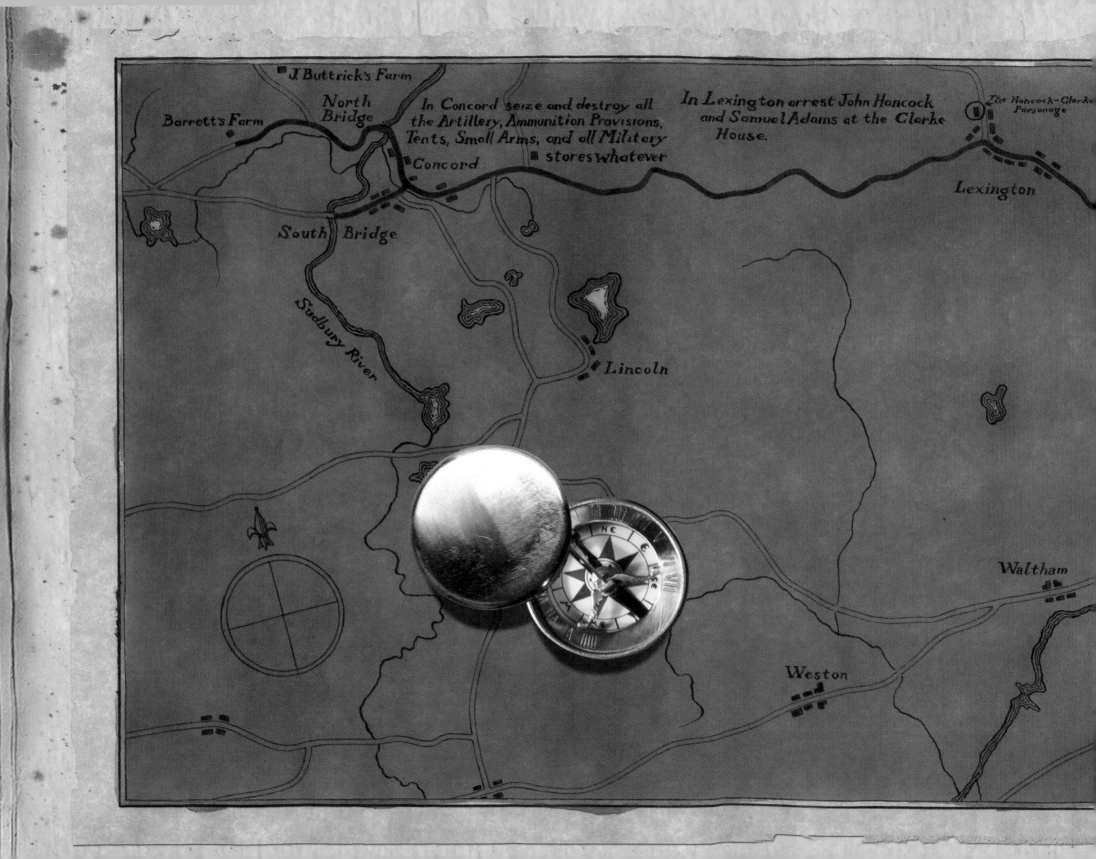

The Plan for the Secret Expedition to Concord

1. The Nantilus Man of War lying above Charles Town Ferry 400 yards to Boſton 2. The Lively Man of War 3. Men of War before Boſton
4. Gen Gage's Camp on the Common 5. Bacon Hill 6. Fort Hill 7. Copp's Hill 8. Gen Gage's line on Boſton Neck 9. The Fortification
10. South Battery 11. North Battery 12. Provincial Battery gained by the King's Troops in the Battle 17 of June 1775 13. Bunkers Hill at
Cha.T. 14. School Hill of Do. 15. Stores of Cannon deſtroyed by King's Troops 16. The Schooner burnt at Noddles Iſland by Gen Putnam
17. Watch Boat 18. Gen Thomas' lines on Boſton Neck

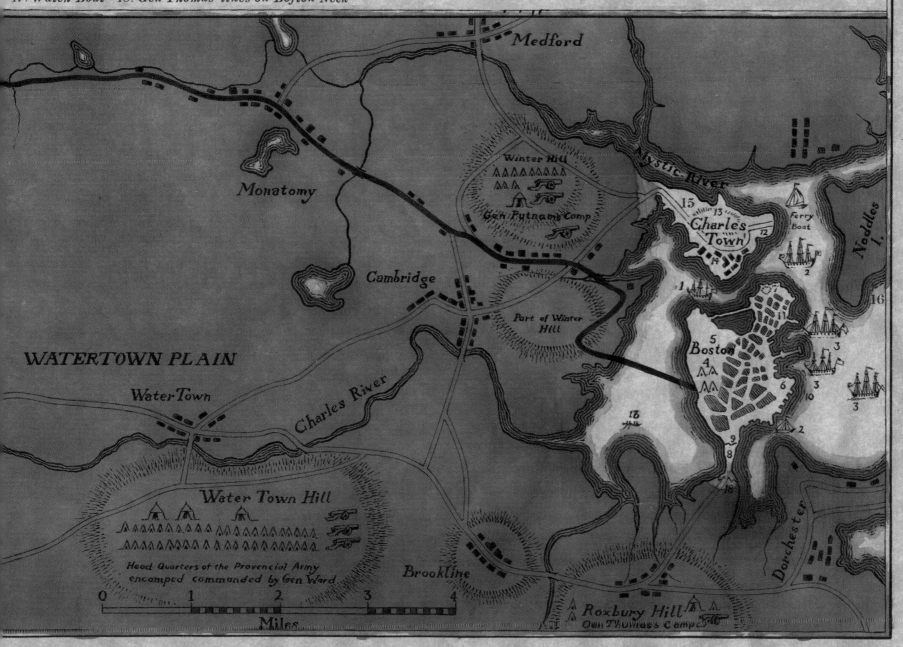

Illustrations © 2001 by Christopher Bing.
All rights reserved. No part of this book may be reproduced in
any form without written permission from the publisher.

Handprint Books is an imprint of Chronicle Books LLC.

Composition and design by Todd E. Sutherland.
Manufactured in China.

ISBN: 978-1-929766-13-0

Cataloging-in-Publication Data is available

10 9 8 7 6 5 4 3 2

Chronicle Books LLC
680 Second Street
San Francisco, California 94107

www.chroniclekids.com

THIS BOOK WAS AWARDED
AS PART OF THE 2009
WE THE PEOPLE BOOKSHELF

PICTURING
AMERICA

Presented by the National Endowment for the Humanities (NEH)
in cooperation with the American Library Association (ALA)

www.neh.gov   www.ala.org

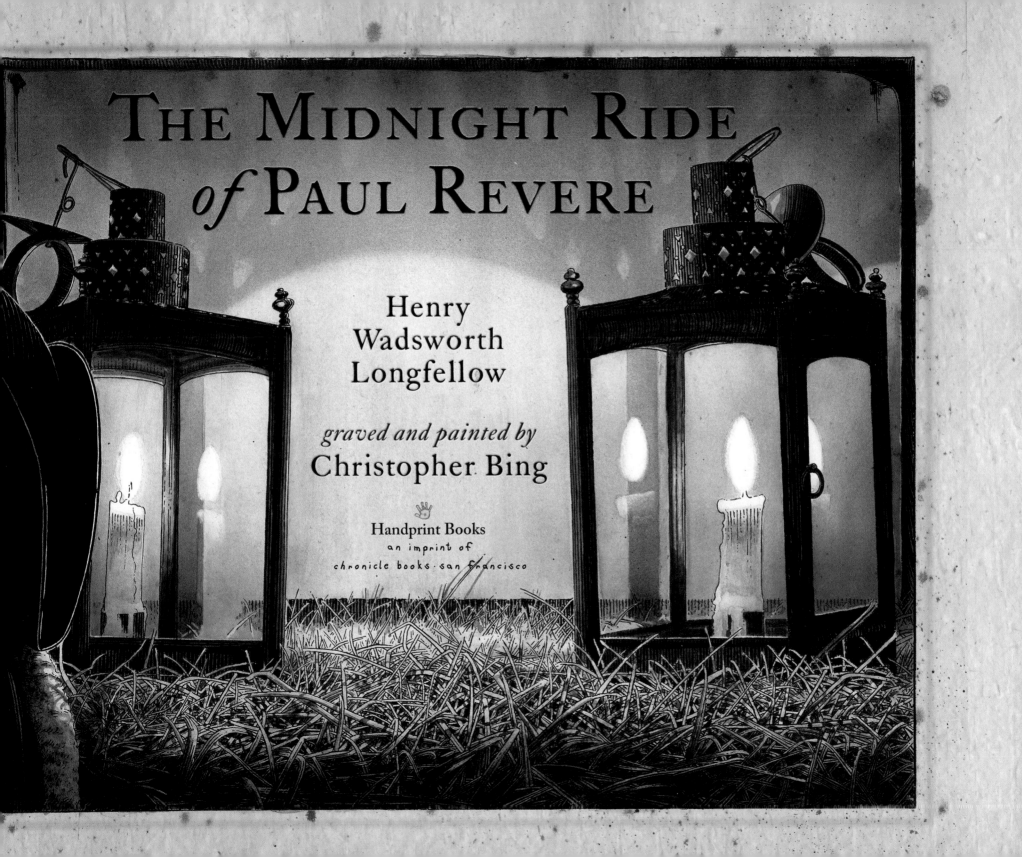

THE MIDNIGHT RIDE
of PAUL REVERE

Henry
Wadsworth
Longfellow

graved and painted by
Christopher Bing

Handprint Books
an imprint of
chronicle books · san francisco

L
ISTEN, MY CHILDREN,
AND YOU SHALL HEAR

Of the midnight ride of Paul Revere,
On the eighteenth of April, in Seventy-Five;
Hardly a man is now alive
Who remembers that famous day and year.

He said to his friend, "If the British march
By land or sea from the town tonight,
Hang a lantern aloft in the belfry arch
Of the North Church tower as a signal light—
One, if by land, and two, if by sea;
And I on the opposite shore will be,
Ready to ride and spread the alarm
Through every Middlesex village and farm,
For the country folk to be up and to arm."

Then he said, "Good night!"
　and with muffled oar
Silently rowed to the Charlestown shore,
Just as the moon rose over the bay,
Where swinging wide at her moorings lay
The *Somerset*, British man-of-war;
A phantom ship, with each mast and spar
Across the moon like a prison bar,
And a huge black hulk, that was magnified
By its own reflection in the tide.

Meanwhile, his friend, through alley and street,
Wanders and watches, with eager ears,
Till in the silence around him he hears
The muster of men at the barrack door,
The sound of arms, and the tramp of feet,
And the measured tread of the grenadiers,
Marching down to their boats on the shore.

Then he climbed the tower
 of the Old North Church,
By the wooden stairs, with stealthy tread,
To the belfry-chamber overhead,
And startled the pigeons from their perch
On the somber rafters, that round him made
Masses and moving shapes of shade—
By the trembling ladder, steep and tall,
To the highest window in the wall,
Where he paused to listen and look down
A moment on the roofs of the town,
And the moonlight flowing over all.

Beneath in the churchyard, lay the dead,
In their night-encampment on the hill,
Wrapped in silence so deep and still
That he could hear, like a sentinel's tread,
The watchful night-wind, as it went
Creeping along from tent to tent,
And seeming to whisper, "All is well!"
A moment only he feels the spell
Of the place and the hour, the secret dread
Of the lonely belfry and the dead;
For suddenly all his thoughts are bent
On a shadowy something far away,
Where the river widens to meet the bay—
A line of black that bends and floats
On the rising tide, like a bridge of boats.

Meanwhile, impatient to mount and ride,
Booted and spurred, with a heavy stride
On the opposite shore walked Paul Revere.
Now he patted his horse's side,
Now gazed on the landscape far and near,
Then, impetuous, stamped the earth,
And turned and tightened his saddle girth;
But mostly he watched with eager search
The belfry tower of the Old North Church,
As it rose above the graves on the hill,
Lonely and spectral and somber and still.

And lo! as he looks, on the belfry's height
A glimmer, and then a gleam of light!
He springs to the saddle, the bridle he turns,
But lingers and gazes, till full on his sight
A second lamp in the belfry burns!

A hurry of hoofs in a village street,
A shape in the moonlight, a bulk in the dark,
And beneath, from the pebbles,
  in passing, a spark
Struck out by a steed flying fearless and fleet:
That was all! And yet,
  through the gloom and the light,
The fate of a nation was riding that night;
And the spark struck out
  by that steed, in his flight,
Kindled the land into flame with its heat.

He has left the village and mounted the steep,
And beneath him, tranquil and broad and deep,
Is the Mystic, meeting the ocean tides;
And under the alders that skirt its edge,
Now soft on the sand, now loud on the ledge,
Is heard the tramp of his steed as he rides.

It was twelve by the village clock,
When he crossed the bridge
  into Medford town.
He heard the crowing of the cock,
And the barking of the farmer's dog,
And felt the damp of the river fog,
That rises after the sun goes down.

It was one by the village clock,
When he galloped into Lexington.
He saw the gilded weathercock
Swim in the moonlight as he passed,
And the meeting-house windows,
 blank and bare,
Gaze at him with a spectral glare,
As if they already stood aghast
At the bloody work they would look upon.

It was two by the village clock,
When he came to the bridge in Concord town.
He heard the bleating of the flock,
And the twitter of birds among the trees,
And felt the breath of the morning breeze
Blowing over the meadows brown.
And one was safe and asleep in his bed
Who at the bridge would be first to fall,
Who that day would be lying dead,
Pierced by a British musket-ball.

You know the rest. In the books you have read
How the British Regulars fired and fled—
How the farmers gave them ball for ball,
From behind each fence and farmyard wall,
Chasing the red-coats down the lane,
Then crossing the fields to emerge again
Under the trees at the turn of the road,
And only pausing to fire and load.

So through the night rode Paul Revere;
And so through the night went his cry of alarm
To every Middlesex village and farm—
A cry of defiance and not of fear,
A voice in the darkness, a knock at the door,
And a word that shall echo for evermore!
For, borne on the night-wind of the Past,
Through all our history, to the last,
In the hour of darkness and peril and need,
The people will waken and listen to hear
The hurrying hoof-beats of that steed,
And the midnight message of Paul Revere.

AN IMMEDIATE SPARK that helped ignite the historic tinderbox the night of April 18, 1775, can be found in a letter written in London on January 27, 1775. The author was Lord William Dartmouth, British colonial secretary, and the letter was directed to General Thomas Gage, governor of Massachusetts and commander-in-chief of the British army in North America. Dartmouth, critical of Gage's inability to quell the rebels fomenting in the colonies, urged the general "to arrest and imprison the principal actors & abettors in the Provincial Congress (whose proceedings appear in every light to be acts of treason & rebellion)."

Two-and-a-half months would pass before that message, carried onboard the HMS *Nautilus*, arrived in the port of Boston on April 14, and was immediately delivered to Gage. While the general vehemently disagreed with Dartmouth's directive, he did not delay in putting it into effect, penning the orders to Lieutenant Colonel Francis Smith of the 10th Regiment, in the letter which is fancifully recreated on the front endpapers.

What actually happened during that night and in the morning of the 19th comes to us from many sources. Few accounts are so direct and forceful as that of Paul Revere, who prepared a deposition, most likely at the request of the Massachusetts Provincial Congress. This body of legislators wished to prove that it was the British troops who had fired first at Lexington. A corrected draft of that deposition, which faithfully preserves Paul Revere's orthography, is recreated on the back endpapers.

That Henry Wadsworth Longfellow took liberties with history is clear. Writing on the eve of the American Civil War, he was consciously creating an American myth and felt free to bend and mold facts to shape a patriotic legend. The careful reader and observer will discern where the paths of history and of Longfellow's interpretation of Revere's ride converge and diverge.

The friend referred to was Robert Newman, the sexton of the Old North Church, who had agreed in the afternoon of April 18 to help with the lanterns. Two other friends of Revere, Thomas Bernard and Captain John Pulling, also offered to help. Revere had arranged to meet them that night at Newman's house. Seeing the British officers, who boarded with the Newmans, playing cards through the front parlor window, Revere waited at the back of the house. He was joined by his three friends, Newman having avoided the officers by pretending to go to bed early and then climbing out of a window.

The British man-of-war, the HMS *Somerset*, was anchored in the Charles River between Boston and Charlestown. Its assignment was to intercept all nocturnal river traffic between the towns. On the night of April 18, the ferries that served the towns were seized and secured alongside the British ship, with "boats, mud-scows, and canoes." River traffic was, in effect, closed. However, Revere managed to evade the British in a small boat with the aid of two skilled boatmen, Joshua Bentley and Thomas Richardson. Legend has it that the men wrapped their oars with a woman's petticoat to muffle the sound of oars grinding against the oarlocks.

At ten o'clock, a selection of General Gage's elite British troops were awakened and told to dress and arm themselves as noiselessly as possible. Leaving their barracks by the back way, they moved so quietly that "no sound was heard but of their feet," and Boston was not alarmed. Their rendezvous was a remote beach on the edge of Back Bay where they were loaded into boats and ferried across the Charles River to Cambridge.

Acting upon their carefully laid plan, Robert Newman, Captain John Pulling, and Thomas Bernard went to the Old North Church. Bernard stood guard outside as Newman and Pulling slipped inside and retrieved the lanterns that Newman had hidden in a closet earlier that day. Although Newman is generally credited with lighting the lanterns and holding them in the northwest window of the steeple in the direction of Charlestown, it is not certain which of the two men, or whether both of them, actually climbed the tower and lit and displayed the two lanterns.

In 1775, the Old North Church was the tallest building in Boston. While the church was easily viewed from Charlestown, there was concern that the light from the lanterns might be too dim to be seen. Most lanterns of the time had sides made of thin, translucent slices of cow horn, which sent out a weak, diffused light. Although the lanterns that Newman used had clear glass lenses, they were no more than a foot or so tall and housed only one candle, which shone none too brightly. It was reassuring to Revere and his colleagues to think that though the light from the lanterns might be difficult to see, it had the best chance to be noticed from the height of the well-positioned Old North Church.

Revere was met at the Charlestown ferry landing by several members of the local militia, including Colonel William Conant and Richard Devens, who assured him they had seen the signal lights. Devens, a Charlestown Whig and a member of the Committee of Supplies, warned Revere to watch for British officers "mounted on good horses, and armed, going towards Concord." A horse named Brown Beauty was made available to Revere.

Brown Beauty had been carefully chosen for Revere by the Charlestown Whigs. It belonged to the family of John Larkin, a deacon of the Congregational Church, and was considered one of the fleetest animals in town. Brown Beauty was an excellent example of a New England saddle horse, known for its size, speed, and strength. Revere was later to write, "I set off upon a very good horse, it was then about 11 o clock and very pleasant."

Revere headed north across Charlestown Neck and then turned west on the road to Lexington. Two British Regulars tried to intercept him, but Revere reversed his course and rode toward the Mystic Road. He outrode one of the Regulars, and the second became bogged down in a clay pit after attempting a cross-country route to cut Revere off. Revere continued toward Lexington on the Mystic Road. Although it took him many miles out of his way, it also kept him safely out of the reach of roving British patrols.

Arriving in Lexington close to midnight, Revere rode straight to the Hancock-Clarke house and parsonage to warn Samuel Adams and John Hancock of the imminent danger. During Revere's time with Hancock and Adams, there was some debate about the purpose of the British troops' mission— whether it was to arrest Adams and Hancock or to seize the colony's stores at Concord. The men decided that the purpose was to seize the stores at Concord, as the expedition was larger than two arrests warranted. As Revere's story has been told over time, "The British are coming!" have been the words attributed to him as he rode through the countryside. However, it is likely that he said, "The Regulars are coming out!" In 1775, most of the people of Massachusetts thought of themselves as British and would have referred to the British troops as Regulars, Redcoats, or King's Men.

Revere stayed in Lexington until one or half past one in the morning. While there he met William Dawes, who arrived in Lexington a half hour after Revere, having followed a southern route out of Boston to give the alarm. As Revere and Dawes rode out of Lexington toward Concord to continue spreading the alarm, they were joined by a young colonist-sympathizer, Dr. Samuel Prescott. Two miles from Lexington Green, the three men were surrounded by ten British soldiers. Dawes and Prescott escaped. In his flight, Dawes was unseated from his horse and made his way to safety on foot. Prescott continued on horseback to Concord, successfully spreading the alarm. Revere, unable to escape, never got to Concord. He was interrogated, searched for weapons, and finally allowed to go free. Brown Beauty was confiscated by the British and was never seen again.

The British Regulars retreated from Concord. Reaching Lexington, the Regulars were saved by the arrival of reinforcements, and after a short rest continued their journey to Boston under constant attack by local militias. Cut off from its planned return route through Cambridge, the Redcoats were forced to retreat to Charlestown. By then, they had been in fierce battle for eight hours and had not slept for two days. The dispirited soldiers were ferried to Boston across the river in longboats.

Americans delight in romanticized versions of the historical hero or heroine, who, entirely alone, bravely battles the forces surrounding him or her. While the Paul Revere who is Longfellow's creation might seem at first glance to fit that image, in reality, Revere can be seen as someone quite different. It is true that he alerted the countryside to the activities of the British. But he did not, as Longfellow says, ride through the entire night, nor did he act alone. Among Revere's great contributions to the American cause was his ability to predict and organize, to plan bold strategies, to form contingency plans, to involve others, and to make effective use of political and social structures already in place. He was a man blessed with a large number of friends and a wide acquaintanceship; he was clearly someone who was greatly respected and who exhibited superb qualities of leadership. How different from the Paul Revere who inhabits our collective national consciousness and how satisfying to encounter not a myth, but a person whose attributes are both human and admirable.

BIBLIOGRAPHY

FISCHER, DAVID HACKETT. *Paul Revere's Ride*. New York: Oxford University Press, 1994. (This book proved especially valuable in the creation of the endnotes).

FORBES, ESTHER. *Paul Revere and the World He Lived In*. Boston: Houghton Mifflin Company, 1999.

HALLAHAN, WILLIAM H. *The Day the American Revolution Began: 19 April 1775*. New York: Avon Books, 2000.

KELLY, C. BRIAN. *Best Little Stories from the American Revolution*. Tennessee: Cumberland House, 1999.

MASSACHUSETTS HISTORICAL SOCIETY. *Paul Revere's Three Accounts of His Famous Ride*. 1976.

REVERE MEMORIAL ASSOCIATION. *Paul Revere: Artisan, Businessman and Patriot: The Man Behind the Myth*. 1988.

TOURTELLOT, ARTHUR BERNON. *Lexington and Concord: The Beginning of the War of the American Revolution*. New York: W. W. Norton & Company, Inc., 2000.

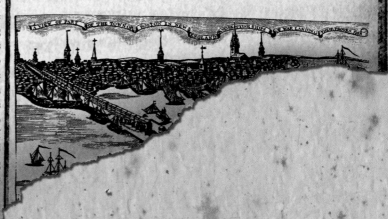

❧ THANKS and ACKNOWLEDGEMENTS ❧

Christopher Franceschelli for suggesting that I consider doing a new treatment of this poem. And for giving me the time to think about it and then not popping his cork as deadline after deadline rolled by. As well as Sally and Anna, who made me feel at home away from home even after stressing their loved one so much.

Carl Brandt, my agent, who laughs at my bad knock-knock jokes, but never at me as I keep him on the phone to get an education. Good health, many laughs and my sincerest thanks.

Todd Sutherland for such brilliant design work in the face of so much resistance. Your heart still shows in the work. Thank you for making my work look so good.

Gina Scauzillo for being only very, very, very touchy instead of very, very, very, very touchy in the face of my faux pas. May you never doubt my respect for your work as Managing Editor (see, I do listen) again.

Juliet Nolan and Ann Tobias who deciphered my notes and spent days checking them against historical sources and shaping them into a coherent whole, and to Helen Chin, whose eagle eyes once again spied more than the occasional error and whose sharp pencil corrected them.

My wife Wendy and our three children, Christian, Amy and Tessa, who go without as I venture into this new world and still keep feeding the bear in the barn with hugs and kisses.

My parents who still have faith in me, and let me know it.

My in-laws Bill and Jean who have suffered in granting me the latitude I needed to complete this project. May you some day read this sentence, nod your heads, and laugh with the certain knowledge that sometimes good things do grow in thick layers of manure. May that day be sooner rather than later.

Patrick Leehey of the Revere House who never hesitated to take or return my innumerable calls and engage me in long discussions of minutiae. It is my hope that you find your dedication, scholarship, and suggestions well represented and respected in these pages. With every intention of being redundant, my thanks.

Carl Hoss of the Old North Church for giving me such unrestricted access to the inside of the Church so I might create the historically accurate images to be found herein. I hope you feel the end result justified your trust. My many, many thanks.

David Connor, the model for Paul Revere in this book, whose passion helps to make history live for so many. His performances around New England, especially at the Revere House and the Old North Church, are not to be missed. May your dreams to make it a year-round, full-time occupation bear fruit. I hope this book will help you to that end. For all the time, patience, labor and help that you so freely gave me, I give grateful thanks.

Mike Lapage, the model for Robert Newman in this book, who suffered greatly facing down one of his fears while modeling for me only to have it all be for naught in the final illustration. Then again, how many people can claim that they had the opportunity to re-enact a pivotal historical event in full dress and know there are photos to prove it? Again, many thanks.

Jerry Chaskes and Winston Stone (First Regiment of Foot Guards) who gave freely of their time and encouragement and were no end of help when I started this project.

D. Michael Ryan, a one-man rebel army who came to my aid in the tradition of the original colonial militias. Many thanks.

Paul O'Shaughnessy (His Majesty's Tenth Regiment of Foot) for his rapid response and help with information regarding the Tenth Regiment of Foot.

Those members of His Majesty's Tenth Regiment of Foot who posed for me on a hot spring day in Lexington and whose names were literally lost to the wind when a gust took the paper they were printed on. My sincere apologies and thanks. I hope you will still feel well represented.

Thomas O. Fenn whose patience will pay off. Thank you for all your help, and the cartridges.

Clint Jackson in Lowell, Massachusetts for his time, suggestions, and recommendations when I first started this project.

All the historical preservationists who participated in the year 2000 re-enactments around Lexington and Concord, especially those who came all the way from the UK only to suffer at the hands of the rebels again.

The Massachusetts Historical Society (Peter, Una, Nick and Jennifer) for their endless patience answering my never-ending questions and for directing me to whom they thought qualified to answer the few questions they couldn't.

Milissa Saalfield of the Minuteman National Historical Park in Concord, Massachusetts for her help in finding photos I could reference and helping me to contact others who could help me in my labors.

The Freedom Trail National Park Service for their help and advice.

Robyn Christensen and The Old State House/Bostonian Society for their kind help and research.

George Cloyed, silversmith in Colonial Williamsburg, for his direction and help in my search for information on silversmiths.

Lorna Congdon and Jeff Wallace with the Society for the Preservation of New England Architecture for their detailed research and quick return of my phone calls.

Kristen Sherman at the Old South Meeting House for making time and room for me to take reference photos.

The American Antiquarian Society in Worcester, Massachusetts.

David Taylor, Michael Lewis, and Simon Stephens of the National Maritime Museum in Greenwich, England, for their help in my research on HMS *Somerset* and the other 1745 Establishment Class Ships.

Barbara DeWolfe, manuscript librarian of the William L. Clements Library, University of Michigan for all her help with General Gage's papers.

All of the staff of the Cary Memorial Library in Lexington for their speedy assistance in my work. My life would be so much harder without them. As usual, all overdue fines will/have been happily paid.

The Boston Public Library and especially Jane Duggan.

Stephen Van Dyke and the kind people at Cooper-Hewitt, National Design Museum Library who were extremely helpful and generous with their resources and personal knowledge on the subject of bookcraft.

This book is for all those historical preservationists who, through labors of love, help recall our past for generations present and future. But this book is ultimately dedicated to my mother Patricia Manhard, who has spent her life teaching social studies to the endless parade of students who pass through her classroom. Her hope is to protect them from the muddy, suffocating riptide of time and history by clarifying the less than 20/20 vision of individual perspective and record passed down to us as fact. She has tempered her instruction with her love of art, which she believes helps mankind survive those things ugly and unwanted in our past.

Paradoxically, she often feels the need to wrest the lies that are legacy and power of art's interpretation of history out of deeply-rooted places in her students' minds in order to replace them with facts as contemporary research and science understand them to be. Such is this offering a mixture of art: one fiction, the other struggling to make its mark as nonfiction. Both with love.

Christopher Bing

A NOTE *on the* PREPARATION *of* THIS BOOK

The artwork, design, and preproduction of this book represents a melding of the old and new.

The artwork was prepared in several stages. Initially the black-and-white foundation illustrations were created with pen, ink, and brush on white or uninked scratchboard. This black-and-white line art was then photocopied onto watercolor paper. Watercolor was then applied over the line images in the traditional method of glazing the colors: first the yellows, next the reds, and finally the blues. The glazing technique is responsible for achieving the "glow" in the nighttime scenes.

The finished illustrations were scanned on a flatbed desktop scanner and interposed with images derived from a myriad of sources including images downloaded over the internet and objects digitally photographed and subsequently manipulated in such programs as Adobe Photoshop and Illustrator.

Ultimately, the digital files which comprise this book were delivered to the printer on five compact disks. It is a testament to the current state of technology that the preparation of this book is truly a desktop production, with no technology used that was not to be found in the artist's, designer's, and publisher's studios.

The body type of the poem has been set in Founder's Caslon 30, one of contemporary British typedesigner Justin Howes's brilliant and accurate digital recuttings of the family of fonts created by the London typedesigner and founder William Caslon (1692-1766). Distinguished by their regularity, legibility, and sensitive proportions, Caslon's typefaces were widely used in the American Colonies. Indeed, the first printed version of the United States Declaration of Independence was set in Caslon.